16th

DRAFT HORSES

DRAFT HORSES

Dorothy Hinshaw Patent

photographs by William Muñoz

HOLIDAY HOUSE/NEW YORK

PHOTO ACKNOWLEDGMENTS

The author and photographer would like to thank the following: Slackpoint Ranch (frontis, pp. 8, 14, 17, 19, 46, 47, 51, 69, 72); Idaho State Draft Horse International show (pp. 2, 19, 23, 31, 45, 51, 52, 53, 54, 55, 57, 62, 73); Ray "Pat" Miller (pp. 4, 6, 9, 22, 24, 24, 49, 67, 69, 75); Clydesdale Auction (pp. 10, 29); Mischka Farms (p. 25); Anheuser-Busch, Inc. (p. 27); Willard Crockett (p. 29); Jerry Hammon (p. 33); David and Beverly Tarmina (p. 41); Forrest Davis (pp. 49, 51, 68, 77); Anderson Shires Farm (pp. 59, 60); Charlie Yerian (p. 63); Roland Moore (pp. 70, 71); Pete Weimer (p. 77); John and Chris Blethen (pp. 13, 35, 36, 37, 38); Fox Valley Draft Horse Farms (pp. 6, 11, 30, 30); Craig and Ingrid Stevenson (p. 41); Martin Fraker (p. 74); Jack Eden and Family (p. 42); Jim and Diane Ellis (p. 12).

Text copyright © 1986 by Dorothy Hinshaw Patent
Photos copyright © 1986 by William Muñoz
Printed in the United States of America
First Edition

Library of Congress Cataloging-in-Publication Data

Patent, Dorothy Hinshaw.
Draft horses.

Includes index.
SUMMARY: Examines the traits, origins, breeds, uses, and care of the big workhorses which have been in use from the Middle Ages to the present.
    1. Draft horses—Juvenile literature. [1. Draft horses. 2. Horses] I. Muñoz, William, ill. II. Title.
SF311.P37 1986   636.1′5   85-21998
ISBN 0-8234-0597-4

For Forrest Davis

Contents

DRAFT
HORSES

*In the old days, coaches like this one transported people
from place to place as buses do today.*

1

The Gentle Giants

Ever since people first tamed them, horses have had a special relationship with the human race. Horses have been teammates in work and comrades at war. They have shared joy and sorrow. No horse has been a more constant companion for humans or a harder worker through time than the big work animals called draft horses. In the Middle Ages, when knights in armor counted on their giant mounts to get them through battle, and continuing into modern times, in which peaceful draft horses share the duties of farming, logging, and other jobs with their human partners, these "gentle giants" have willingly given their energy and companionship to people.

Draft horses played important roles in the development of the United States. They were once the key element in the success of American business and agriculture. Before automobiles, trucks, and tractors became common, horses were

Farmers today have refurbished old equipment like this potato harvester.

the main source of power for all sorts of vehicles. They pulled delivery wagons for coal, wood, ice, and other products, and they tugged streetcars from place to place. Powerful draft horses galloped down the streets during emergencies, drawing life-saving fire engines. They worked on the railroads, on road construction, and in clearing the forests.

As American agriculture developed, horses became more and more important in increasing the efficiency of human labor. In the mid-1800s, it took three hours of human work to produce a bushel of wheat, from planting to harvesting. Thanks to horse-drawn farm machinery, only an hour of human labor went into a bushel of wheat by 1900. A good draft horse can accomplish the work of ten men, while its room and board costs only half that of just one person. Even today, we evaluate an engine by computing its "horse-power."

Engine power came around in the early 1900s and by mid-century, it had taken over from horses. In 1918, there were 27 million horses and mules in the United States, a high percentage of which were heavy work animals. In the 1940s, during World War II, manpower was in short supply, and tractor power was available. This combination hastened the decline of draft horses on the farm, for using horses requires more human labor than running a tractor. By 1960, which was the low point for horses in the United States, there were only 3 million of these animals left, and most of them were lighter-weight riding horses, rather than heavy drafters. So few horses were left on the farm in 1960 that the official count of farm horses was then discontinued.

Using Horses Today

Fortunately, a few hardy horse lovers kept breeding and sometimes using heavy horses during those years of unpopularity, so drafters did not disappear completely. Besides scattered farmers across the country, the Amish people, who live largely in Pennsylvania and Ohio, refused to abandon horses in favor of motors and kept real horsepower alive and well. Then, during the 1970s, more and more people began to realize that there were uses for these powerful animals even in the modern world. On northern ranches in the wintertime,

When draft horses were out of favor, fortunately some people continued to raise them so they did not die out.

Draft horses are used to pull a hay wagon for cattle during the winter.

the cattle must be fed hay every day. While trucks and tractors often refuse to start in the cold, horses are always ready to go and can pull a wagon or sleigh loaded with hay through the snow with ease. Farm machinery is very expensive, and a small farm often doesn't produce enough to make buying it economical. During the 1970s, farmers began to realize that sometimes horses could work more inexpensively than machines. Horses cost far less than machinery, and hay is less expensive than gasoline. The manure produced by horses goes back to the soil to fertilize the fields. If grain doesn't sell, it can be fed to the horses. Besides, no tractor can generate offspring to replace itself the way a good mare can.

Working with horses has other benefits, too. A tractor is noisy and smelly, and the vibrations of the engine can rattle one's bones. Riding the seat on horse-drawn equipment is another story. The only noises are the gentle clopping of hooves into the ground, the jingling of the harness, the soft sound of the turning soil, and the songs of birds singing nearby. The air smells of the earth instead of gasoline. Now and then there are bumps and bounces, but mostly the rig glides and dips over the ground. There is time and peace to enjoy the beauty of the land, and horses make fine, feeling companions that can never be duplicated by a piece of machinery.

In the old days, people had no choice. If there was hard work to be done, horses were needed. Nowadays, however, a farmer can choose between machines and animals. Those who decide to use horses must be willing themselves to work harder, for horses are slower than machines and require more care. The horses must be harnessed before starting out and

Working with horses is peaceful, quiet work.

unharnessed, fed, and washed after work. But for people who love animals, the teamwork between human and horse provides deep satisfaction.

With the renewed interest in draft horses today there are not only more animals at work but more animals used for recreation. Farmers take neighborhood children for wagon and sleigh rides. Rebuilding old wagons is popular with many draft horse owners, and in some areas, modern-day wagon trips are part of the fun. Families join together and travel overland, through less populated areas, to share a sense of adventure and enjoy the company of one another and the horses.

Just like other people, draft horse owners also enjoy competing with one another to see whose animals are the strongest or best looking and to find out who can handle a team

Children always enjoy a ride behind lively horses like these Percherons.

most skillfully. Draft horse shows have more and more entrants every year and provide a place to meet people and horses, share knowledge, and enjoy the excitement of competition.

Some draft horse people enjoy reliving the past by rebuilding old wagons and going on overnight trips together.

What Is a Draft Horse?

The term "draft horse" applies to a particular size and type of animal. A typical riding horse weighs about a thousand pounds and stands 15 to 16 hands high. (A horse's height is measured in "hands," with a hand equaling four inches. The height is taken from the ground to the top of the shoulder, called the withers. If a horse is said to be 15.3 hands, that means that it is 15 hands and 3 inches tall at the withers.) An average draft horse, on the other hand, weighs in at almost 2000 pounds and stands over 16 hands tall. Not only are draft horses big, they are built differently than pleasure horses.

Draft horses are big, powerful animals.

Their legs are shorter in comparison to the rest of their bodies, their chests are wider, their bodies are rounder, and their necks are shorter and thicker. All these differences spell power, for draft horses are much more heavily muscled than riding horses. After all, their function in life is to work, often pulling extremely heavy loads. Their muscles are thick; thick muscles are more powerful than the long thin ones that give breeds like Thoroughbreds their breathtaking speed. Draft horses also have big hooves to support their heavy bodies.

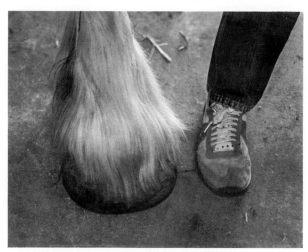

A human foot is small compared to that of a draft horse.

Another general trait of draft horses is their gentle, willing disposition. A workhorse that won't obey quietly is worthless and potentially dangerous, no matter how strong it is. With the driver separated from the animal by long lines instead of a saddle, controlling it depends greatly on its willingness to cooperate. A good draft horse must be able to pull hard when necessary and stand around and wait, sometimes for hours, between jobs. Because of their gentleness, draft horses are often very good with children.

Clydesdales have long legs for draft horses.

The uses to which they were put helped determine the shape and size of the different kinds, called breeds, of draft horses. Breeds such as the Clydesdale were employed mainly for pulling heavy wagonloads, often on slippery cobblestone city streets. The heavier the horse, the more gripping power it had on the road, so these breeds were developed for large size compared to riding horses. Long legs allow for an easy, fast walk or trot, so breeds used for pulling loads were selected for long legs. Short legs, however, have more pulling power, and many farm uses require getting heavy loads on the move efficiently. For this reason, breeds like the Suffolk, which came about purely as a farm worker, have very short legs. Short legs also make the animal more surefooted and stable as it moves over uneven ground.

The world has a great variety of heavy draft horse breeds, but only a few are popular in the United States. The Belgian, Percheron, and Clydesdale are most common, with Shires and Suffolks increasing in numbers. Smaller breeds of strong horses, such as the Fjord and Hafflinger, are also often used for draft purposes. Mules, too, are good work animals, especially when the mother horse is a drafter.

Suffolks have short legs.

Draft Horse Origins

The ancestors of almost all European draft horse breeds came from northern Europe. Belgium is a small country northeast of France, which has two different regions. In southern Belgium, French is the language while in the northern area a language similar to Dutch, called Flemish, is spoken. Even before recorded history, large strong horses seem to have lived in this area. These powerful black Flemish horses existed before the time of Julius Caesar, who was impressed by their size and strength. They may have developed from a uniquely European prehistoric horse that was heavier than the type which led to lightweight horses such as the Arabian.

The deliberate breeding of large, heavy horses in Europe really became important during the Middle Ages. At that time, knights wore heavy armor to protect themselves from the spears of their enemies. Not only did the knight himself

The strength of the draft horse can be seen in this Belgian mare.

wear armor, so did his horse, as the knight was helpless if his mount was killed or seriously wounded. By the time the weight of the armor, weapons, saddle, and rider were added up, a horse ridden by a medieval knight had to carry well over 400 pounds. Only big strong horses could bear that weight, so native horses in different countries were bred with the Flemish horses to produce large, heavy animals. The resulting Great Horse, which could carry knights in battle without faltering, was the magnificent predecessor of most modern draft breeds.

Only specially trained stallions were ridden into war by knights. These valuable animals were called destriers. Since they were aggressive stallions, the destriers could not be put to graze with the other horses and required special care. Only at the last moment before battle did the knight mount his destrier, which was led by hand while the knight rode a smaller, more comfortable horse called the palfrey. Because of their own weight and the weight they had to carry, the destriers could not canter or gallop for long distances. They could trot, but the trot is hardly a comfortable gait for the rider, even on a lightweight saddle horse. The gait of the destrier was so painful that trotting in full armor by the hour was used as a punishment for knights in need of discipline.

Because the horses were so valuable and because possessing the best heavy horses gave a nation a great advantage in war, each king tried to keep such animals from being exported, and each country went into the business of breeding its own Great Horses. Thus, after some Flemish horses were imported into England to add weight and strength to horses there, the British bred their own heavy mounts, which became ancestors of the Shire and the Clydesdale.

2

Draft Horses from the European Continent

In Europe there are many kinds of draft horses. Each country has its own work breeds, all of which probably owe much to the ancient Flemish black horse. Native lightweight horses and sometimes Arabians influenced these animals so that each breed has its own special characteristics. But only two kinds from the European continent, the Belgian and the Percheron, have been brought into the United States in large numbers.

Belgians

The most popular draft horse in the United States today is the Belgian. In Belgium, there is more than one breed of draft horse. The Brabant, also called the Belgian Heavy Draft Horse, is the biggest and most common draft horse in the

Flemish part of the country and is the result of centuries of selective breeding from the original Flemish horse. It is a powerful, rounded horse with a broad chest, short back, and short legs. It has quite a bit of feathering—long hairs—on its lower legs. Another Belgian breed, the Ardennes, is smaller and faster than the Brabant. The draft horses in Belgium are very heavily muscled and have big bones and short legs. They are well-suited to hard work in the fields. Belgian horses can be any of several colors. Some Belgians are black or gray. Bay—reddish brown body with black mane, tail, and lower legs—is also typical. Roans—horses with white hairs

A Belgian

mixed in with the basic body color, giving the animals a gray-ish look—are very common, too. The white hairs are not evenly distributed, so the coat of a roan horse looks shaded rather than all the same color. Chestnut Belgians are found in Belgium as well. A chestnut horse has a yellowish coat, which can be light or dark. When it is dark reddish yellow, it is sometimes called sorrel. Chestnut horses often have lighter manes and tails.

In the United States, Belgians have been bred since 1866, and by 1887 an association was formed to keep track of American Belgians. Horses were bred here and also imported up until World War I. The war and the economic depressions that followed it reduced importation of horses. Interest in Belgians was high, however, even around this time. In 1917, the year America entered the war, a Belgian stallion named Farceur sold for the incredible sum of $47,500, a fortune in those days. Despite inflation, that is still the highest price paid for a draft horse in the United States.

By the mid-1930s, breeding of Belgians was going strong, and horses were again imported, since work animals were still used on most farms. In 1937, more Belgians (3,196) were registered in the United States than in any year before or since until the 1980s. World War II brought an end to imports when Germany invaded Belgium in 1940. Since then, few, if any, Belgians were imported until the 1970s.

These animals were bred for many generations in the United States, where traits different than those in Belgium have been emphasized. Chestnut horses with light manes and tails are preferred here. Although roans and occasionally other colors are sometimes seen, the majority of American

A Belgian mare and foal

The Belgian is especially gentle and reliable.

Belgians are chestnuts, often with almost white manes and tails. White blazes often decorate their faces. Our Belgians are less massive than their cousins in Belgium, and their legs are longer, with less feather. The less feathering a draft horse has, the easier it is to keep its legs clean, especially on a farm.

Generally speaking, however, even though they are not as massive as their ancestors, Belgians are the heaviest of the draft horse breeds for their height in America. The heaviest horse ever, in fact, was a Belgian stallion named Brooklyn Supreme, which weighed 3,200 pounds and stood 19.2 hands tall. Belgians usually weigh between 1,700 and 2,200 pounds and stand at 16 to 18 hands.

Belgians have a reputation for being the calmest and gentlest of all the draft horse breeds. They are also "easy keepers," requiring modest amounts of food to perform plenty of hard labor. In addition to being willing farm workers, Belgians are especially strong. Despite the breeding for longer legs, these handsome horses are still lower to the ground than other breeds and are thus especially adept at getting heavy loads underway. When contests are held to see how much weight a team of horses can pull, Belgians are likely to come out on top. The world weight-pulling record for horses (4275 pounds) is held by a pair of Belgians.

Percherons

The Percheron is in some ways the beauty of the draft horse world. With a build somewhat lighter than the Belgian, the Percheron often has an especially handsome head, arched neck, and graceful body—results of the addition of Arabian Horse blood. The Percheron originated in a region of France called La Perche. The Moors from North Africa, who used Arabian Horses, conquered Spain in 711 A.D. and ruled western France briefly. After they were defeated, Arabian stallions taken from them were bred with local animals and again, during the Crusades, Arabians were brought back from the East by the conquering Christians. Much later, in the eighteenth century, Arabian stallions were once more brought to France to improve the Percheron.

Like the ancestors of the Belgian, the forebearers of the Percheron carried knights into battle. Later, they pulled large coaches owned by noblemen or were used for carrying passengers; then they became farm workers. The first Percherons were imported into the United States in the 1850s, before systematic breeding had begun in France. The Percheron Horse Society of France was organized in 1883 and allowed only horses actually born within the boundaries of La Perche to be registered as true Percherons. La Perche is only slightly larger than Rhode Island, so large numbers of horses cannot be produced there. In addition, the two world wars interrupted importing of Percherons as much as of Belgians. American Percherons, then, like American Belgians, were bred independently from the animals in their original homeland. Only as recently as 1983 were a few Percherons again imported directly from France into the United States.

In the early days, Percherons were the most popular draft horse in the United States, for several reasons. For one thing, when a Percheron stallion was bred to a lighter weight mare, the resulting horse was big and powerful enough to be used for draft work. By such crossbreeding, many strong horses could be produced by importing just a few stallions. Percherons also could stand heat well. These traits, combined with their versatility, made Percherons the draft horse of choice for many years.

Percherons are powerful and elegant.

The influence of the Arabian horse can be seen in the graceful head of the Percheron.

This gray Percheron mare will get lighter in color as she gets older.

Percherons are good all-around workers.

Percherons are almost always gray or black. All the foals are born black. Those that will turn gray as they grow older usually have some light hairs at birth. The older the gray horses get, the lighter they usually become, with some turning almost white. Percherons average 16 to 17 hands in height, and stallions generally weigh about a ton. They show good "action"—that is, they pull their knees up when they walk or trot so that their hooves rise high off the ground. This gives them a very flashy look, especially when they are all fitted out for a show. Their action and faster gaits make Percherons more suitable for pulling big loads over distances than Belgians, and their great strength enables them to get a heavy load underway and pull it farther than Clydesdales or Shires. These abilities make them an especially good all-around draft animal. Percherons are generally more spirited than the quiet Belgian, but they are also good-natured and willing workers. Like American Belgians, Percherons have little feathering on their legs, making it easy to keep them clean.

A spirited Percheron stallion

3

British Breeds

Britain boasts three distinct kinds of draft horses, all of which have been brought across the sea to America to work the land—the Clydesdale from Scotland, and the Shire and Suffolk from England. Each has its own special traits that make it valuable to those who use, show, and breed it.

Clydesdales

Thanks to the famous Budweiser beer hitch team, the Clydesdale is the most familiar draft horse in America. The Budweiser team (owned by the Anheuser-Busch Company) came about at the end of Prohibition in 1933. For years, alcoholic beverages had been outlawed in the United States. So when beer became legal again, August A. Busch, Jr., bought a team of Clydesdales to celebrate the end of Prohibition. Before trucks, draft breeds such as Clydesdales had been es-

The Budweiser Clydesdales come to town.

sential to the success of breweries, for their great strength enabled them to pull wagons heavily laden with beer. Clydesdales were especially effective as wagon horses because their relatively long legs gave them faster gaits than more short-legged breeds. The Budweiser horses proved so popular that the company began raising them itself. As draft horses began to fall out of favor in the 1940s, the Anheuser-Busch farm became one of the major forces in keeping these animals from disappearing from the American scene, and the frequent appearances of the Budweiser horses at fairs and parades kept drafters in the minds of the American people. Today, Anheuser-Busch maintains three different hitches—sets of horses, harnesses, and a wagon—one in St. Louis, one in New Hampshire, and one in California.

Giant Clydesdales, with thick silky feathering on their legs flowing as they pick their feet up high with striking action, are a breathtaking sight as they trot by. With each step, the horses lift up their knees high enough so that each horseshoe flashes in the sun. Clydesdales are lighter in build than other draft breeds, usually standing 16 to 16.5 hands tall and weighing from 1600 to 1900 pounds. The Budweiser Clydes are taller than most, at 18 hands each. The basic color is roan, bay black, or dark brown, with various white markings. All the Budweiser Clydes are bays, with four white legs and a white blaze on the face. Because of the popularity of their flashy action, Clydesdales with four white legs bring more money than those with less white on the legs. White blazes or stars on the face are also common, as are additional white markings on the belly.

Unlike Percherons and Belgians, Clydesdales have been steadily imported into both the United States and Canada over the years. For this reason, American and Scottish Clydesdales are not significantly different.

The Clydesdale originated in the region of the River Clyde in Scotland. The breed began with stallions imported from Belgium from 1715 to 1720 that were bred to the smaller, local workhorse mares. English Shire horses may also have been used at this time, but early on, introduction of other horses was discouraged as the Scottish strove to develop their own distinctive, beautiful breed of draft horse. Clydesdales were used for hauling coal from the local coal fields and for hauling heavy loads in the city of Glasgow.

These horses have always been especially popular for pulling wagons because of their energetic, tireless trot and

Even when moving slowly, the Clydesdale lifts its feet high.

Clydesdales are not as powerfully built as other draft breeds.

snappy action. No other draft breed can trot as fast as a Clydesdale, so they have always been able to deliver goods faster than the others. But Clydesdales are not as popular on the farm as Belgians and Percherons, partly because of their thick feathering and frequently white legs. It is difficult to keep their legs clean, and the heavy hair can harbor diseases and parasites. In addition, their longer legs and lighter build make Clydes less suitable to getting heavy loads on farms underway. Even so, quite a few farmers do enjoy using these somewhat spirited but good-natured animals in their fields.

The famous Clydesdale action can even be seen in the foals.

Shires

Although individuals of other breeds can be very big, the English Shire is overall the largest of all horse breeds. Shire stallions commonly reach 18 hands and over, averaging 17 to 17.1 hands, and regularly weigh more than a ton. Like other draft breeds, the Shire traces to the Flemish horse and to the Great Horses that carried knights in battle. As a breed, Shires can be traced back at least as far as 1755 to a stallion referred to as the Packington Blind Horse. A hundred years later, the Shire Horse Society was formed, and breeders concentrated on improving the breed, resulting in the beautiful Shire of today.

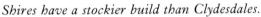
Shires have a stockier build than Clydesdales.

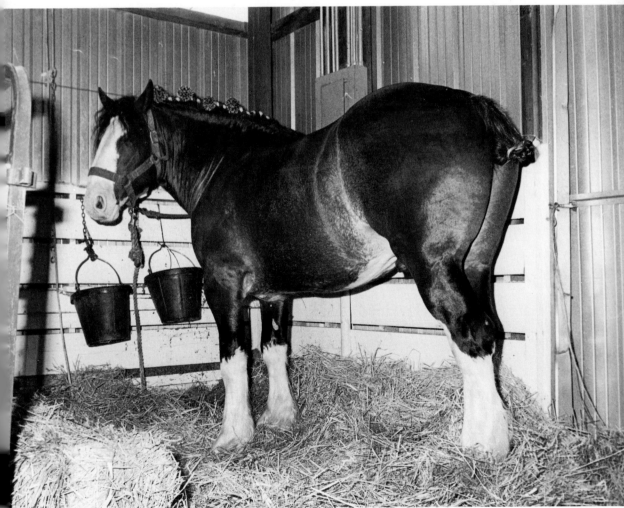

While the Shire resembles the Clydesdale superficially, there are important differences between the two breeds. Shires are bigger and have heavier bones than Clydes, and until recently, the Shire was generally a more sluggish, unrefined horse. Old-style Shires have shorter legs relative to their height than do Clydesdales, and they are not as spirited.

In the early days in America, the Shire was the third most popular draft horse breed, with more than 400 Shires imported in the peak year of 1887. But because of its slowness, the Shire was not as popular as an all-around farm animal as were Belgians and Percherons. Shires were more popular in cities, where their heaviness and strength allowed them to pull very heavy loads without strain. Just leaning all that mass into the collar got the load underway without jerking. Those early Shires also had a great deal more feather than do Shires today. They even had tufts of hair growing from the front of each knee. The Shire's feather is coarser than that of the Clydesdale and led to more problems of infection when the animals were used on the farm, where dirt and mud are unavoidable.

The feathering on a Shire's legs can be quite long. Breeders sometimes oil the feathering on their show horses to keep the hairs from breaking so it can grow as long as possible.

A six-horse hitch of black Shires is an impressive sight.

In the United States today, Shires are again gaining in numbers. In 1967, the first registered stallion in 30 years was imported, and in the early 1980s dozens of British Shires, some fine champions, were imported to improve the breed in America. A team of jet black Shires, each with three or four snow-white, feathered legs, makes an impressive sight when working together to pull a show wagon. Because of the Shire's great show possibilities, many breeders today are aiming for a more elegant looking, spirited animal than the old-style Shire. With their tremendous size, these more refined giants are an impressive sight indeed. The new-style Shires retain the friendliness, gentleness, and willingness to work that characterize this breed.

Black is a popular Shire color that provides a striking contrast to the pure white feather desired on their legs. Shires also come in bay, gray, brown, and occasionally roan. In the United States today, Shires are still quite rare, with fewer than 400 registered animals. In 1983, 41 Shires were imported, more than in any other year since World War I. This contrasts with the early years of this century, when 3,907 Shires were imported between 1907 and 1917.

Shires are sometimes gray, like this mare.

Suffolks

There are fewer Suffolks in the United States than any of the other major draft horse breeds. The Suffolk (sometimes called the Suffolk Punch), from Suffolk County, England, is especially interesting, however, for it differs from the other kinds of draft horses in several ways. For one thing, all Suffolks can trace back to a single stallion called "Crisp's Horse," born in 1760. This remarkable animal was a bright-colored chesnut (for some reason, the "t" is left out of the word "chesnut" when applied to Suffolk horses) that stood only 15.2 hands but was extremely strong. The Suffolk of today looks remarkably like the descriptions of "Crisp's Horse" and his early descendants, except that it may reach

A newborn Suffolk. Suffolks are increasing in numbers both in America and in Britain.

16.2 hands. Some claim that the Suffolk can be traced back even further, to the early 1500s, which would make it by far the oldest breed of British draft horse. All are chestnut in color, with a range extending over seven different shades, from an almost black-brown to a golden sheen. Often, Suffolks have very light manes and tails, and sometimes they have small white markings on the head and legs. Unlike the other two British draft breeds, Suffolks have very little feathering on their legs. Suffolks are very gentle and friendly with people.

A Suffolk.

Even Suffolk foals have big bones and compact bodies.

The general appearance of a Suffolk is even more compact and muscular than that of other draft horse breeds. Unlike them, this animal was developed for farm work and has always been used in that way. They usually weigh from 1600 to 1800 pounds, although stallions standing barely over 16 hands may weigh over a ton. Suffolks, especially stallions, have a very short, thick strong neck which carries a rather small, refined head. Their legs are short and their bodies very rounded. They are powerful pullers, with especially muscular shoulders and hind legs.

Despite their ability to work so hard, Suffolks do not require very much food for their size, another desirable trait. They also grow fast and can be used for work at a relatively young age. Suffolks live longer than most other horses and can work and bear young well past the time other horses have been retired to the pasture. Suffolks in their 20s are still working and having foals, and occasionally a mare in her 30s is still producing offspring. Another advantage of the Suffolk is its ability to go out "on the road," pulling a wagon from place to place and eating only the roadside grasses without needing grain or other feed brought along for it.

4

Other Draft Animals

While big heavy horses can do all sorts of work that is difficult or impossible for smaller animals, great size can sometimes be a disadvantage. For one thing, big horses eat more than small ones, so they are more expensive to keep. On a small farm, a smaller animal or team may well be able to carry out the necessary work and be less costly to keep. In addition, the largest draft horses are not able to maneuver as well as smaller ones in the close quarters of jobs such as logging. A strong small horse is also more versatile, for it can be ridden comfortably as well as used in harness. For all these reasons, other animals besides the big breeds are also used for many of the same jobs. Here are samples of the alternatives—the Norwegian Fjord Horse, the Austrian Hafflinger, and the mule.

Norwegian Fjord Horse

The Norwegian Fjord (FEE-yord) Horse is popular not only in Norway but in the other Scandinavian countries as well. This powerful, compact, pony-sized horse has existed since prehistoric times, with its image engraved on rocks thousands of years ago by unknown artists. The Fjord horse is very distinctive looking. Its 13 to 14 hand-tall, half-ton body is very stocky, and its neck is quite thick. All Fjords are dun in color—that is, their bodies are a shade of tan, with dark feet and occasionally stripes on the legs. A dark stripe also runs down the center of the upright mane and down the back into the tail.

Fjord horses can live on very poor pastures, a great advantage in their often rocky, mountainous homeland. They are sure-footed and gentle, and are especially easy to train for work. Even stallions, which in other breeds can be difficult to work with, often need very little training to become useful helpers. Because of their small size, these animals also are comfortable riding horses and can go for long distances at a tireless trot. Many people believe the Fjord horse comes the closest to perfection of all horses. It is beautiful but practical, gentle but hard-working, and can be used for any purpose a horse is good for. Fjords thrive on little food, only needing meager rations even during the cold winter months. They are especially strong, too. A Fjord pulling team in Canada consistently was able to beat draft horse teams that outweighed it by hundreds of pounds. There are only about three hundred Fjord horses in the United States and Canada, but their numbers are growing every year as more people learn about this friendly and versatile animal.

Two Fjord horse foals playing.

The Fjord horse has a distinctive black stripe that runs from the forelock, down the middle of the neck, along the back, and into the tail.

The Hafflinger

The Hafflinger comes from the mountains of Austria and southern Germany, where it performs many different tasks. It plows the mountainside fields and carries loads up and down the slopes on its broad back. The Hafflinger is a popular riding horse, too, for despite its small size, it has a long, easy stride that makes for a comfortable ride. In the mountains, the sure-footedness and toughness of the Hafflinger are a great asset. Its hard hooves are a match for steep rocky paths. Hafflingers are still quite rare in America, but their numbers are increasing both in the United States and Canada as more people discover this versatile breed. A typical Hafflinger stands only 13.3 hands tall, weighs about 1,000 pounds, and is chestnut in color, with a light mane and tail. It has a strong body and a handsome head. All Hafflingers trace back to Arabian ancestors, which helps account for their beauty. Hafflingers are useful on small farms, for they eat less than half as much as a big draft horse yet perform more than half as much work.

A Hafflinger

Mules

When a female horse is mated with a male donkey, the resulting animal is called a mule. A mule inherits the long ears, thin tail and mane, and small, hard hooves of its father along with the greater size and strength of its mother's body. Mules, as a rule, cannot themselves reproduce (very rarely, a female mule is reported to have given birth), but mules are such hardy, sure-footed animals that many farmers and mountain packers prefer them to horses for work. In general, mules are stronger for their size, have more endurance, need less food, and are more resistant to disease than horses.

When a large mule for draft purposes is desired, a draft mare is bred to an especially large donkey called a Mammoth Jack. While a draft mule is not as powerfully built as a draft horse, it is a hard worker that can survive on meager feed. Draft mules range from 16 to 17.2 hands tall and weigh from 1200 to 1600 pounds. Since mules are tolerant of the heat, they are especially popular in the South. Their sure-footedness and maneuverability also make them good for logging work.

Mules help collect the hay bales that will be used to feed them during the winter.

5

Caring for Draft Horses

While working with draft horses is less expensive in the long run than using a tractor, the horses require much more time than does machinery. A tractor needs to be serviced much like a car—it needs oil and gas, and now and then it may require some repairs. Horses, on the other hand, are living things. They need to be fed and given water every day. Their coats and hooves require attention. And before they can be used, they must be harnessed up so that their great power can be channeled into useful work.

Feed

During most of the year, horses can get a good deal of their food from grazing in the pasture. In addition to grass, however, horses also need hay and grain, especially when work-

The feathering of Shires and Clydesdales need to be washed to keep them clean.

Belgians feeding in winter.

A foal licks a salt block. Horses need minerals in addition to grass, hay, and grain. The salt block contains other important minerals in addition to ordinary salt.

ing or pregnant. Workhorses are usually given their hay and grain, such as oats, in three meals, just like people, with the largest meal in the evening after they have finished working. In the wintertime, horses in the North must be fed plenty of hay, since the grass in the pasture isn't growing.

Farmers usually raise their own hay for feeding their horses and other animals. The horses actually help raise their own food by their work in the fields, and the manure they make is used to fertilize the crops. Thus, both the labor and the wastes of the horse's body help go to producing food for it.

Hooves

A horse's hoof is like a gigantic toenail, although it is more complicated in structure. Like a toenail, the hoof keeps growing, so it needs to be trimmed. In the springtime, the horses are brought one by one to have their feet checked over and their hooves trimmed. This can be quite a project, especially with young horses that haven't been handled often. The horse must be restrained and its foot tied while the long edge of the hoof is trimmed off and the hoof filed down to evenness.

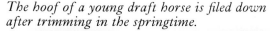

The hoof of a young draft horse is filed down after trimming in the springtime.

Harnesses

The harness used with draft horses looks very complicated, but every part has an important function. While harnesses vary in details, certain important pieces are always there. The key part of the harness is the collar that goes around the neck of the horse and rests on its shoulders. The horse itself is actually pushing on the collar when it moves forward, not pulling. The pushing of the horse causes the collar to pull against the harness, moving the load forward. The collar must be carefully fitted for each horse so it is comfortable.

Around the outside edge of the collar is a groove into which the pair of hames fits. Each hame is made of wood and/or metal. After being nestled into the groove in the collar, the hames are joined around the top and bottom of the collar by straps. Each hame has a snap or bolt about two-thirds of the way down on which the traces attach. The traces are heavy leather straps that attach at the other end to whatever is being pulled by the horse or team. The place where the traces are attached to the hames is called the point of draft, for it is where the pulling power of the horse is tapped.

There are also three metal rings on each hame through which the lines of the harness pass. The driving lines pass from the bit in the horse's mouth and through the top pair of rings on the hames to the hands of the driver. The breast strap is snapped onto the bottom rings. It is a wide, strong piece of leather that helps keep the load from hitting the back legs of the horses when they are backing up, slowing down, or going downhill. The backstraps go through the top set of

Harnessing draft horses takes time. Here you can see the collar and the right hame. The right trace is attached to the hame and runs through a loop on the bellyband. The breast strap is snapped onto the bottom ring on the hame, while the backstrap is attached to the middle ring. The top ring, through which the driving line passes, is covered by the rope attached to the halter.

The back part of the harness. The lines passing over each horse's rump make up the hip drop assembly, which holds the broad leather band, called the brichen, in place under the horse's tail.

rings. They are attached to a set of straps that pass over the rump of the horse. These straps, called the hip drop assembly, can be adjusted and serve to support another heavy piece of leather, called the brichen or breeching, in place. The brichen passes around the rear of the horse, under the tail. It is loose while the animal is pulling but presses against the horse while it is backing up, helping move the load backward.

The harness has other parts besides those concerned with moving the load. The back pad, for example, which fits where a saddle would, provides a place for attaching the bellyband. The bellyband passes under the horse's belly and has a heavy loop on each side. The traces run through these loops so that they are kept from moving too far up along the side of the horse. If the traces were to be pulled up, they would force the bottom edge of the collar into the throat of the horse, choking it.

On its head, the draft horse wears a bridle that looks similar to the one worn by a saddle horse. Sometimes leather flaps along the sides of the bridle act as blinkers that restrict the horse's vision so that it can only see forward and down. Blinkers are supposed to keep the horse from being distracted or frightened by activities going on next to it or behind. The halter, a headpiece of cloth straps to which a lead rope can be fastened, is often left on the horse's head under the bridle. That way, when there is a break in the work, the bridle can be removed and the horse can easily be tied up.

The harness used for everyday work is practical and quite plain. For show, however, bright rings, fancy buckles, and other decorations are often added. Show harness can be quite

Horses often wear blinkers to keep them from being distracted while they work.

A work harness is often very simple.

expensive, costing from $1,500 to as much as $2,500 for each horse, while working harness costs no more than about $800 for an entire set.

Two horses that work side by side are called a team. The horses harnessed together to pull a load are called a hitch. Horses are linked in different ways to form a hitch, depending on how many horses there are and how they are arranged. Usually, when two horses are used, they are worked side by side. In the old days, on very narrow streets, two horses were hitched one in front of the other. Four horses are usually hitched in two pairs, one in front of the other, especially when pulling wagons. For some sorts of farm work, however, when more power and an even pull on equipment working a wide area is used, the animals are hitched up four abreast.

A show harness is decorated.

6

Competing

Competition is a part of being human. People want to know how they stand against others, and they want to know the same thing about their animals. Spectators love the excitement of competition and enjoy trying to figure out on their own who will be the winner. Draft horse owners are no different from other people when it comes to competition. They are proud of their horses and of their own skills, and they enjoy being tested.

Shows

Draft horse shows are becoming more and more popular every year. While conformation classes are held at shows, in which the animals compete to see which ones best meet the standards of appearance for their breed, the most exciting part of a show is the performance competition.

ANNUAL
IDAHO   STATE
DRAFT & HORSE
INTERNATIONAL
WELCOMES YOU

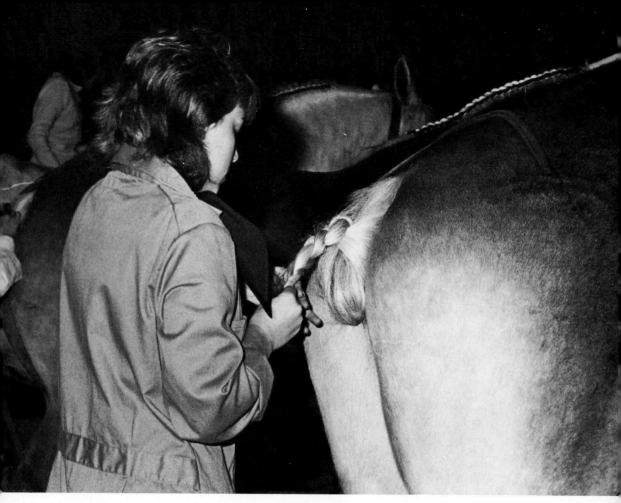

In Junior Showmanship, boys and girls compete to see who can do the best job getting a horse ready for show as fast as possible.

Before horses are shown, their manes and tails are carefully braided to show them off to best advantage. Originally, there were different ways of braiding the manes and tails of the various breeds of draft horses. The goal in braiding up the tail is to show off the powerful muscles of the animal's rump. As the manes are braided, tassels are attached at intervals to emphasize the graceful curve of the strong, arched neck.

At the Idaho State Draft Horse International show, held in Sandpoint, Idaho, annually since 1976, the number of entries

This handsome Percheron takes a peek out of its stall at the fairgrounds during a show.

has increased greatly each year. Even in the flashy show categories, where a wagon can cost as much as $15,000, a dozen or more hitches of six or eight horses may be entered, with over two dozen entries in the less glamorous farm team class. There is a special category for senior team driving, in which older farmers who have worked with horses all their lives can compare their skills, and a junior cart class, in which future farmers can gain valuable experience under pressure.

The junior cart class is judged 100 percent on driving ability. The beauty of the horse and the quality of the cart do not matter, only the skill of the young person driving the horse. Boys and girls of all ages compete here and must show their proficiency at controlling their horses at different gaits and getting them to turn and back up on command.

The judge watches as the driver backs his horse during the junior cart class competition.

Forrest Davis is on his way to a blue ribbon in the hitch-team class. His well-matched Percherons are moving in harmony with one another.

In the hitch-team competition, the ability of the team to work together is most important. The two horses should look as much alike as possible and should be so in tune with one another so that they perform as much like one horse as possible. The driver needs considerable skill in making the horses respond well to commands and in helping them perform together in harmony.

In the four abreast class, the conformation of the horses is considered, so the entrants choose their best-looking horses. How the animals work together and how well they move at different gaits is also important in the judging.

A beautiful team of Belgians competes in the four-abreast class.

The most impressive sights at a draft horse show are the big hitches of four, six, or eight horses pulling together. The largest horses are usually hitched closest to the wagon. They are called the wheel team and must do most of the pulling. The front team is called the lead team and usually consists of smaller, faster horses since they must travel farther when the hitch makes a turn. When there are six horses, the team in the middle is called the swing team. With eight horses, the extra pair is added between the swing and lead teams and is called the point team.

A team of four Shires hurries away from the arena, for two more horses must be added quickly to compete in the next class at the show.

When a judge watches hitches in action, he looks closely to see that all the horses are doing their share of work so that the traces are all tight. The animals must cooperate well during turns, slowing down or speeding up so the turn is smoothly executed. It takes a great deal of skill on the driver's part, too, to control so much horsepower and to help the animals do their best.

It takes quite a few people to change a four-horse hitch into a six-horse one in a hurry.

The six-horse hitch moves with grace around the area.

Pulling Contests

A very popular kind of competition for draft horses is a pulling contest. In this competition, the sheer strength of a team is pitted against the competition. Pulling contests have three weight divisions. In the lightweight category, the team weighs no more than 3,000 pounds. Middleweight teams total under 3,400 pounds, while heavyweights are over 3,400 pounds. Sometimes, pulling contests are run using a machine called a dynamometer that measures the pulling force of the team. But more often, a sled is weighed down with 100-pound bags of grain. Each team takes its turn at pulling the weight. A peg attached to a ten foot length of rope is tapped

The judges watch carefully for the peg to pull up, indicating a successful pull, while another team waits in the background.

Charlie Yerian, a veteran champion at pulling contests, urges his team of Belgians on. Notice that the horses are working well together.

into the ground just behind the sled. When the team has pulled ten feet, the peg comes out of the ground, and the judge blows a whistle. The team has successfully pulled the weight and can go on to the next higher weight. Each team is allowed three attempts, if necessary, to succeed.

At each round, 300 or more pounds is added to the load. The contestant who pulls first gets to choose how much weight will be added. As the pulling proceeds, teams drop out as the weight gets to be too much for them. When the contest approaches the end, teams may be able to pull the load partway, but not the entire ten feet. Then the distance pulled is measured, and the team moving the farthest wins.

When a team has won its category, it is allowed to move up to the next division. When horses are really good, they can often win out over far heavier teams. Teamwork is very important in pulling, for if both horses do not work together, they will fail, no matter how strong they are. The driver is very important in helping the horses work as a team.

The horses appear to enjoy the competition as much as the people do and get more and more excited the heavier the load becomes. Sometimes towards the end of the competition, the drivers have trouble keeping their horses quiet until they are properly hitched to the load and ready to pull. Teams in pulling contests commonly pull well over twice their weight, with winners sometimes pulling two-and-a-half times what they weigh or even more.

7

Working

Draft horses are designed for work, and it is as working animals that they have their most important functions. Horses can perform a number of different tasks, from plowing to logging and even to helping lift the logs used in building a log house.

Farming

The small farm is where the draft horse comes into its own as a "using" animal. With a pair of horses, a farmer has the power needed to get the work done. In the springtime, the soil in the fields must be worked to make it ready for planting. There are several stages in preparing the ground for planting. First, it must be plowed to loosen the soil. With a simple plow, the farmer holds the handles while the horses pull. A riding plow allows the farmer to sit and guide the

Two Percherons pull a hand plow.

horses. During plowing, one horse walks in the furrow that was made in the last pass over the field while the other horse walks on the unplowed land. Some horses are better than others at being the "furrow horse."

Next, the clods of dirt need to be broken up and the ground smoothed for planting. Disking loosens the soil and breaks up most of the clods. Harrowing is another way of breaking up clumps of soil and smoothing out the ground after disking. A harrow is a wide piece of equipment with

After plowing, the soil is disked.

teeth that dig into the surface. A spring tooth harrow has teeth on the ends of rounded springs that stick up above the ground. A spike tooth harrow has teeth on the underside. When the ground is all smoothed out, it is time to plant. Many different types of planting equipment are available.

Horse farmers often believe in doing their work as naturally as possible. They prefer to use manure, a natural fertilizer, instead of modern chemical ones. Chemical fertilizers may only provide the nitrogen, potassium, and phosphorus

Harrowing. Notice the soil across the lower right corner, which has already been harrowed, is smoother than the rest of the ground in the picture.

plants need to grow. Manure, on the other hand, contains trace quantities of other important nutrients and also adds organic matter to the soil. That organic matter helps keep the soil loose and allows it to hold water much better than soil that has been fertilized only with chemicals.

Horse farmers generally grow a lot of hay, since that is their "gasoline." Horses can draw the equipment necessary to cut, bale, and gather up the hay, so they contribute to growing, harvesting, and collecting their own food, something a tractor never does.

Planting corn. The long arms out from the sides of the planter guide the farmer in spacing the rows.

A team of Belgians takes a break while gathering hay.

Even when it is −30° F, horses are ready to go to work.

Winter Feeding

One of the most important roles for horses on the farm or ranch comes in the wintertime. Horses and cattle in the fields must be fed hay every day, no matter what the weather is like. Tractors are hard to start up when it is very cold, but horses are always willing to go. When the snow is deep, tractors can bog down, but horses can keep pulling and move the wagon or sled reliably. Even ranchers who use tractors to perform other chores often keep a team of draft horses around to help with the winter feeding.

Horses can do anything a tractor can as long as the right equipment is available. As more and more farmers turn back to horses, old equipment designed for horses has become harder and harder to find. Ingenious people, however, have found ways of adapting tractor equipment to horses, and a few manufacturers are now making farm machinery specifically to be used by horses. Clearly, farming with horses is here to stay.

Hay is unloaded from the wagon to feed the cattle.

Logging

Horse logging has a very important place in our ecologically aware society. Logging with machinery is most effective in clear-cutting, when all the trees in an area are removed, leaving large, bare patches scarring the land. Selective logging, in which only the biggest trees are removed, can be done to some extent by machines, but the very size of logging machinery means that large areas are scarred, even when some trees are left standing. With machinery, an eight-foot-wide path must be gouged across the ground to each tree that is felled, and the remaining trees are often scraped by the dragged logs, damaging them so that insects or diseases can harm them more easily.

Mules are useful in logging because of their agility.

A team of Percherons in logging harness. Draft horse shows sometimes feature competition in skidding logs.

Horse logging, on the other hand, can economically be done on a small scale. Most of the logging in the northeastern part of the country is selective logging on small plots of land, so horse logging is especially effective there. With horses, dragging the logs can be more carefully and accurately done so that the standing trees are not damaged. Instead of cutting large swaths through the woods over which logs are dragged, trails only as wide as the team of horses can be used to drag the logs out, and the horses can weave between the trees so as not to damage them. And even when logs have been dragged over the paths many times, the plants underneath are not completely destroyed. Horses are also useful for bringing in logs from a small woodlot that a homeowner uses as a source of wood for home heating, and they can be used to clean up fallen trees after a storm.

A pair of Fjord horses hauls a load of wood through the snow.

Buying and Selling

While horses can be bought directly from their owners, auctions are a popular way to sell drafters and farm equipment. Auctions attract not only people interested in buying but also people who like to watch horses in action and those who love a good show. After a horse or team has been shown to the crowd, bidding starts. If bidding is slow, the auctioneer tries to encourage people to bid more money by telling everyone how fine the animal or the equipment is. Mares often sell for good prices, for they can produce more horses as well as work. Attractive, well-trained teams can also bring in good money. Auctions are a way of distributing many horses to new owners in a short time, a useful method when the draft horse business is expanding. They also allow newcomers to see many horses at once and to learn what makes a good working animal.

Percherons show their skill at pulling a wagon at an auction.

Teaching and Learning

Draft horses must be trained to know their roles when used in the fields. To train a new horse, it is hitched up with experienced animals that help it to move in the right way at the right time. While the driver can pass commands to the horses along the driving lines and use voice commands, horses that have been working for some time know what is expected of them and often do the right thing automatically. Some maneuvers can be tricky, and the horses must work together with one another and with the driver towards the common goal.

As more and more people decide to use horses for work, they too must learn how to use the animals. Like any other occupation, working with horses involves many different types of knowledge. Not only are there many new skills to learn, there are many dangers that must be avoided. In order to pass knowledge on from experienced workers to new ones, classes are held at farms that use horses to teach the techniques of working with horses to newcomers. In addition, field days during which many horse owners get together and pool their knowledge and skills help give people a chance to learn more about this quiet and productive way of getting work done.

*Making a corner requires knowledge on the part
of both the horses and the farmer.*

*Forrest Davis watches while a student learns
to drive a team four abreast.*

Draft Horse Publications

Small Farmer's Journal
3890 Stewart St.
Eugene, Oregon 97402

The Evener
29th & College
Cedar Falls, IA 50613

The Draft Horse Journal
Box 670
Waverly, IA 50677

Sources for More Information

Belgian Draft Horse Corporation of America
P.O. Box 335
Wabash, IN 46992

Clydesdale Breeders of the United States
Rt. 1, Box 131
Pecatonica, IL 61063

Hafflinger Registry of North America
14640 State Rt. 83
Coshocton, OH 43812

American Donkey and Mule Society
Rt. 5, Box 65
Denton, TX 7620

The Norwegian Fjord Horse Association of North America
29645 N. Callahan Road
Round Lake, IL 60073

Percheron Horse Association of America
Route 4
Columbus Road
Fredericktown, OH 43019

American Shire Horse Association
14410 High Bridge Road
Monroe, WA 98272

American Suffolk Horse Association
15B Roden
Wichita Falls, TX 76311

Glossary

Ardennes: A breed of draft horse found in Belgium that is smaller and faster than the Brabant.

back pad: A part of the draft horse harness that fits where the saddle would sit.

backstraps: A pair of straps that connect the collar to the hip drop assembly.

bay: A horse with a reddish brown body and black legs, mane, and tail. Some bays have white on their legs.

Belgian: The most popular draft horse breed in the United States today, which came originally from Belgium.

bellyband: A strap that runs from the back pad down under the belly of the horse.

blaze: A white stripe down the center of a horse's face.

blinkers: Flaps of leather attached to the bridle that keep a horse from seeing to the sides.

Brabant: The most common breed of draft horse in the Flemish part of Belgium; it is descended directly from the ancient Flemish horse.

breast strap: A wide piece of leather that passes across the chest of a draft horse.

breed: A particular kind of animal, such as a Belgian draft horse, that produces predictable traits when bred to another of its kind. To be officially a member of a particular breed, an animal must usually have parents who belonged to the same breed, and its birth must be registered with the breed association.

brichen (breeching): A heavy piece of leather that passes around the rear end of a draft horse and helps move the load when backing.

bridle: A headpiece of leather straps which holds the bit, a piece of metal in the horse's mouth used to direct the animal.

chestnut: A golden colored horse, often with a lighter mane and tail. Chestnuts range from a light yellow to a deep reddish gold.

Clydesdale: A draft breed from Scotland with relatively long, feathered legs.

crossbreeding: Mating an animal of one breed with one from a different breed.

destrier: A medieval Great Horse stallion trained for riding into battle.

disking: Turning the soil with a piece of machinery that digs into the ground with a set of turning disks.

driving lines: The long leather straps that pass from the bit in a horse's mouth to the hands of the driver and through which he or she controls the horse or horses.

dun: A tan horse with dark legs, mane, and tail, and a dark stripe down the back.

dynamometer: A machine used to measure how much weight a team of horses can pull.

feathering: Long hair found on the legs of some horses, especially prominent on Shires and Clydesdales.

Flemish horse: The earliest recognized draft horse, originally found in the Flemish part of Belgium.

foal: A baby horse.

forelock: The tuft of hair between a horse's eyes.

furrow horse: The horse in a farm team that must walk in the furrow that has already been plowed.

Great Horse: A strong, heavy type of horse that carried medieval knights into battle.

Hafflinger: A breed of small strong horse from the mountains of Austria often used for draft work.

halter: A headpiece of cloth or leather to which a lead rope can be snapped.

hames: Two pieces of wood or metal that fit into the sides of the collar and to which rings that hold many parts of the harness are attached.

harness: The collection of leather straps that allow the power of the draft horse to be transferred to equipment such as a plow or wagon.

harrowing: Smoothing out the ground using a piece of equipment with many teeth.

hip drop assembly: A set of harness lines that pass over the rump of a horse, holding the brichen in place.

hitch: All the horses used together to pull a load. A hitch may consist of several teams.

lead team: The front team in a four, six or eight horse hitch.

mane: The long hair down the back of a horse's neck.

mare: A female horse.

mule: A cross between a male donkey and a female horse.

Norwegian Fjord Horse: A strong, small horse from Norway that can be used as a draft or riding horse.

palfrey: The horse that was ridden by a knight to a battle scene, before he mounted his destrier.

Percheron: A breed of black or gray draft horse from France.

point team: The team between the swing and lead teams in an eight-horse hitch.

roan: A horse that has white hairs mixed in with the basic color of its coat.

saddle horse: A horse used for riding.

Shire: A breed of draft horse from England with lots of feathering on its legs.

sorrel: A reddish chestnut colored horse.

stallion: A male horse.

Suffolk: A British breed of draft horse with short legs and a very compact body.

swing team: The middle team in a six-horse hitch, and the team between the wheel and point teams in an eight-horse hitch.

team: A pair of draft horses hitched together.

traces: The heavy leather straps that join the collar to the load being pulled.

wheel team: The team closest to the wagon in a hitch of four or more horses.

withers: The top of a horse's shoulders.

Index